Hugging God

Written & Photographed by
Gale Nemec

Special Thanks
Anne Bailey
Andre

Copyright © 2011 Gale Nemec
All Rights Reserved
ISBN:10:1466447184
ISBN- 13:978-1466447189

DEDICATION

This book is dedicated to Mom and Dad who took us to Sunday school and church nearly every single week and thus gave us a life-long love and joy for hymns, a deep faith and a strong belief in God/Christ.

What do you see in this photo?
A cat? A dog? A pig?

This book belongs to:

_____

The date today is:

_____

Hugging God

Written & Photographed by
Gale Nemec

Two people were talking.
One person asked the other,
"What are you doing?"

The second person answered,
"I'm hugging God."

And the conversation continued . . .

"You can't hug God . . . He's too big!"

"I know.
But I'm doing it anyway."

"How?"

"Like this . . ."

"Ahhh. You're just spreading your arms and closing your eyes."

"I know.
But I'm spreading them out very wide – as wide as they will go."

"Gee! That's pretty wide."

"I know.
I spread my fingers, too. As far as they can spread!"

"Golly, that's a lot."

"I know.
Then I close my eyes."

"Why? That seems silly."

"I know.
But with my eyes closed I can feel God hugging me, too."

"Hey! How do you know He is hugging you??"

"Because my whole face smiles and my insides feel happy, and I know God is hugging me, and holding me, and carrying me and that He will get me through!"

"I never thought of that. But wait a minute . . . what if you are sad? I bet you don't feel God hugging you then."

"Yes, I do."

"How?"

"When I'm sad, I close my eyes and some how I feel a smile inside of me and I KNOW God is with me, and that He will hold me and hug me and will be with me until I feel happy and smile again on the outside."

"That happens when you are sad?"

"Yes.
Do you know what happens when I open my eyes?"

"No."

"Everywhere I look, I see hundreds of things made by God. When I listen, I hear them, too."

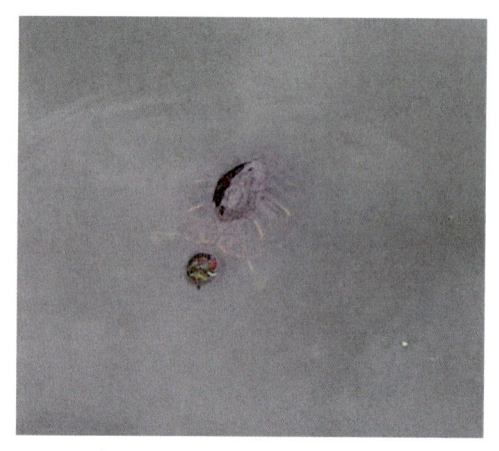

"Yeah? Like what?"

"The petals on the flowers.
The leaves drifting down.
The colorful cars, the busy streets . . .
I just look around.

The singing birds,
the climbing squirrels,
all the people, too.

The barking dogs,
the meowing cats.
Look what God can do!

The sound of the rain,
the brilliant sun,
the sparkle of the snow.

The thunder's roar, the floating clouds.
There's so much to hear, see and know."

"Ummm . . . can I hug God?"

"Sure! Let's hug God together! Spread your arms as wide as you can and stretch your fingers, too. Now close your eyes and don't say a word and you will feel God hugging you!"

"I can feel Him! I can feel Him! I can feel His hug, too! My insides are bright, happy, smiling and light! I am hugging God and He is hugging me, too!"

"I know."

*The Beginning. . .
not The End.*

*You can hug God right now!
Stretch your arms, spread your
fingers, close your eyes and
hug God.*

More picture books you will enjoy written & illustrated by Gale Nemec

Gale Nemec Books
www.GaleNemecBooks.com

Email:
GaleNemecBooks@gmail.com
ChildrensStoriesWithMizzNemec@gmail.com

Little Stockey & the Miracle of Christmas

There's A Bear on A Bench

The Great Elephant Rescue

Throwing Rocks in the River

No Valentines for Trevor or Emily

Valentines for you the Whole year Through

Valentines' for Valentine's Day

Trevor and the T's

Benjamin Loves the Beach

Read-along CD
"Little Stockey & the Miracle of Christmas"

Draw or write down the things you see that are made by God. If you don't know how to draw or write ask someone to help you. Send your discoveries to me at: GaleNemecBooks@gmail.com or to my website: www.GaleNemecBooks.com

_____

_____

_____

_____

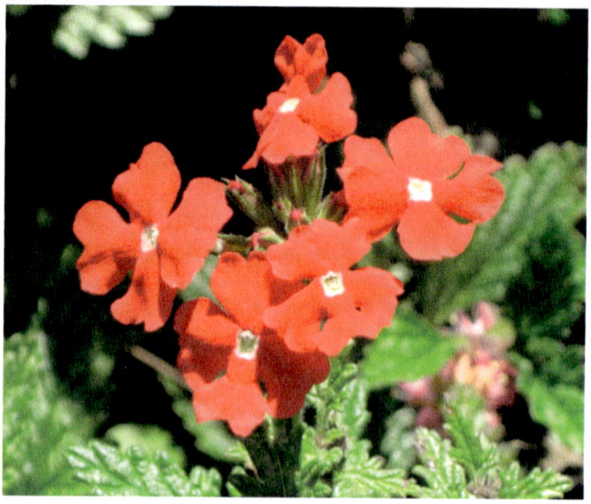

God Loves You

Made in the USA
Middletown, DE
11 December 2021